FIRST GRAPHICS | BODY SYSTEMS

A Tour of Your Nervous System

by Molly Kolpin
illustrated by Chris B. Jones

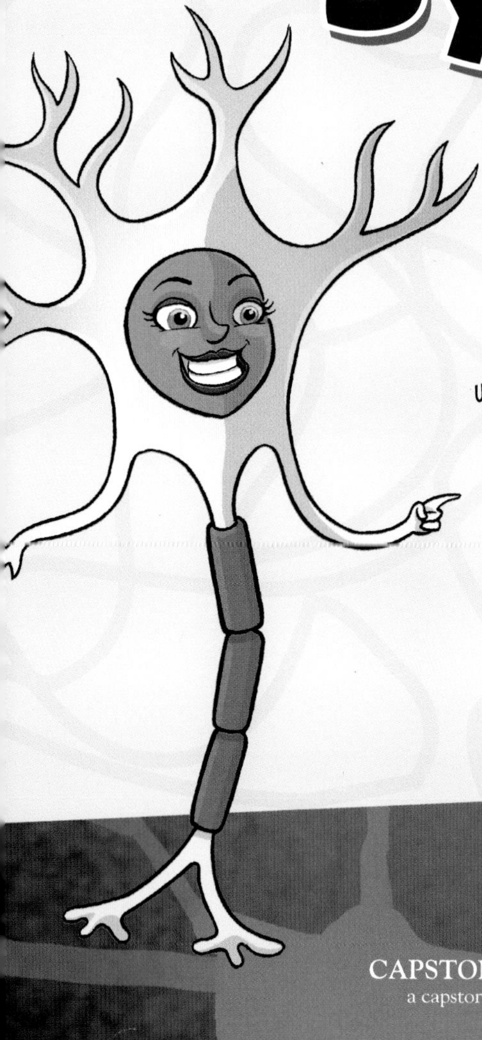

CONSULTANT:
Marjorie J. Hogan, MD
Associate Professor of Pediatrics and Pediatrician
University of Minnesota and Hennepin County Medical Center
Minneapolis, Minnesota

CAPSTONE PRESS
a capstone imprint

First Graphics are published by Capstone Press,
1710 Roe Crest Drive, North Mankato, Minnesota 56003.
www.capstonepub.com

Library of Congress Cataloging-in-Publication Data
Kolpin, Molly.
A tour of your nervous system / by Molly Kolpin ; illustrated by Chris B. Jones.
p. cm.—(First graphics. Body systems)
Summary: "In graphic novel format, follows Nelly Neuron as she travels through
and explains the workings of the human nervous system"—Provided by publisher.
Includes bibliographical references and index.
ISBN 978-1-4296-8739-3 (library binding)
ISBN 978-1-4296-9328-8 (paperback)
ISBN 978-1-62065-264-0 (ebook PDF)
1. Nervous system—Juvenile literature. I. Jones, Chris B., ill. II. Title.

QM451.K65 2013   2011051828
612.8—dc23

Editor: Christopher L. Harbo
Designer: Lori Bye
Art Director: Nathan Gassman
Production Specialist: Kathy McColley

Printed in the United States of America in Stevens Point, Wisconsin.
012013   007145R

Table of Contents

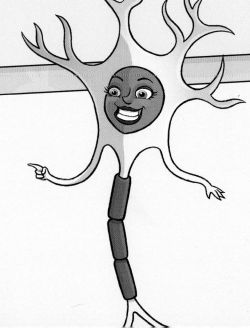

The Nervous System

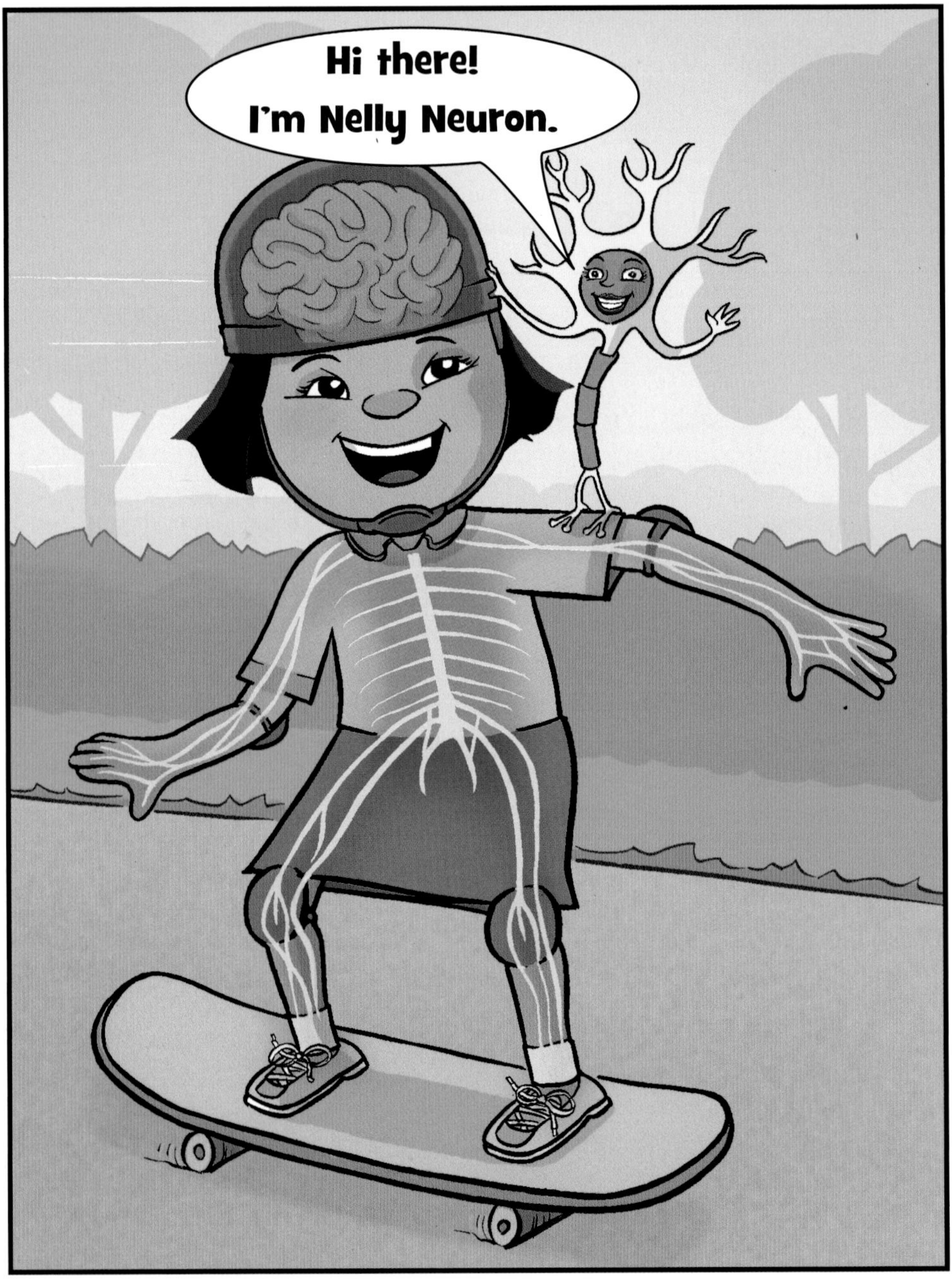
Hi there!
I'm Nelly Neuron.

I'm about to travel through the nervous system.

The nervous system tells your muscles when to move.

It also tells you when something is hot.

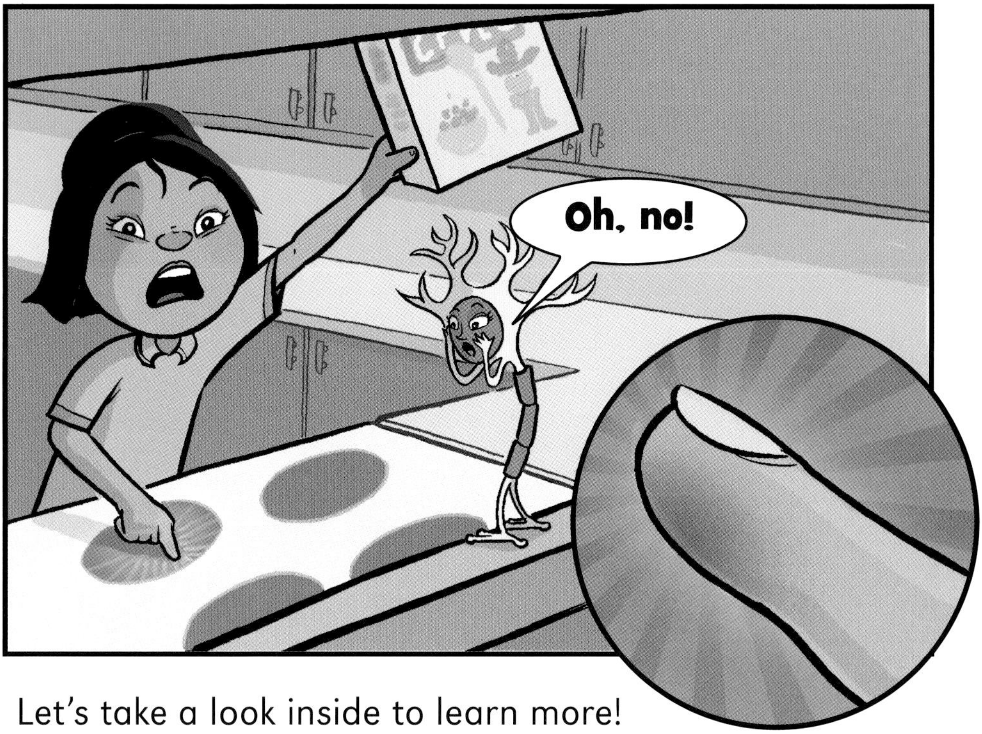
Oh, no!

Let's take a look inside to learn more!

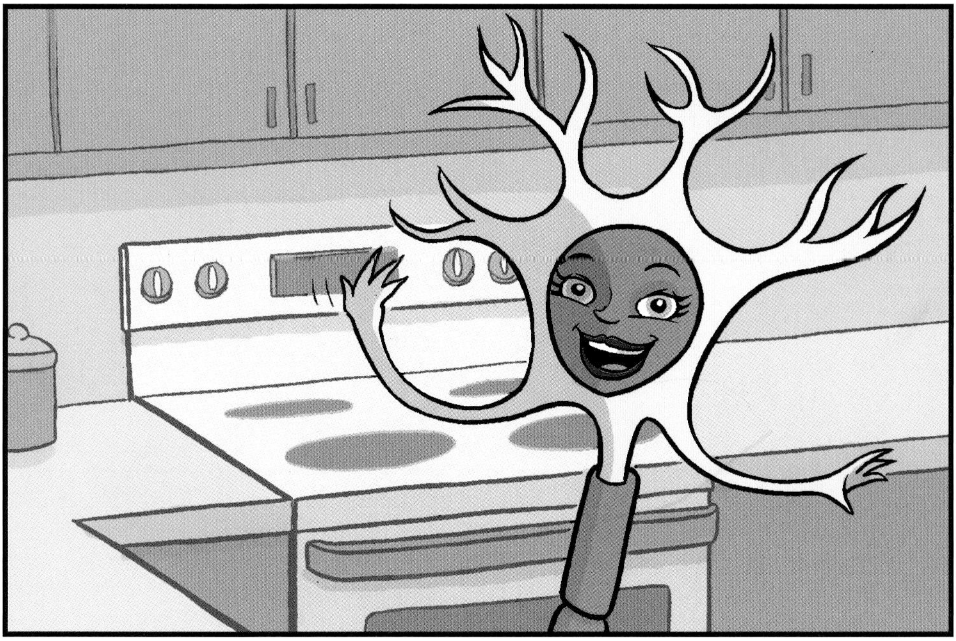

The Neuron Network

Every move you make starts with neurons.

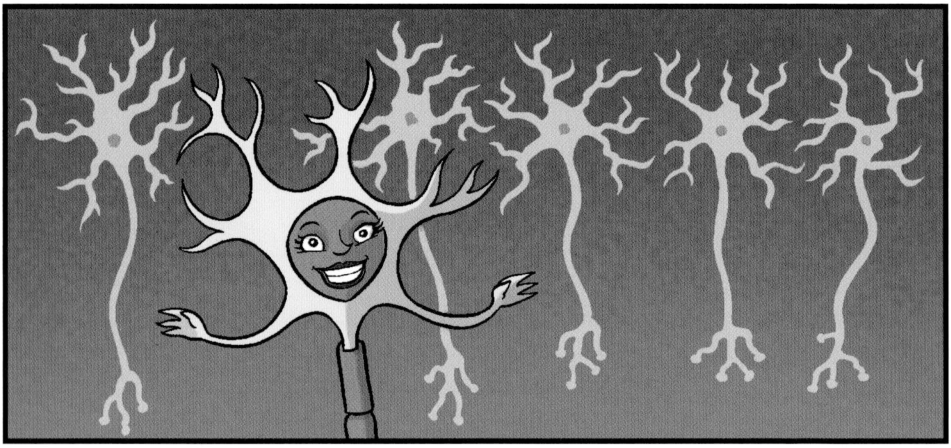

Neurons are tiny cells inside your body.

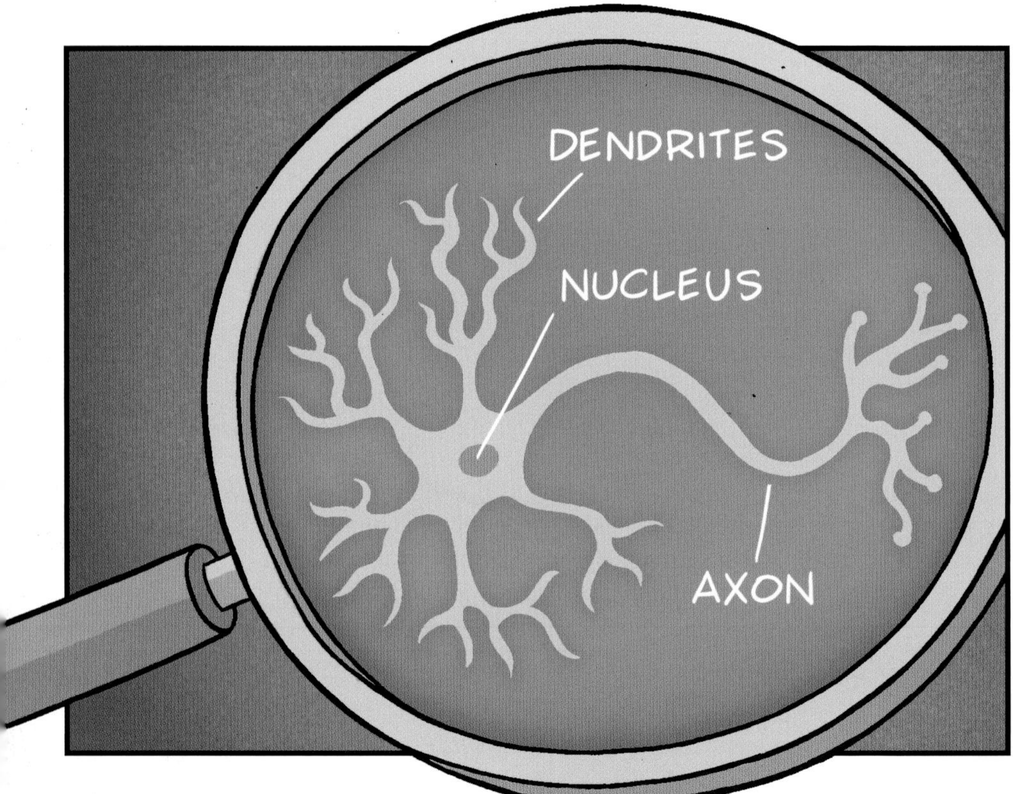
DENDRITES
NUCLEUS
AXON

These cells pass messages to each other.

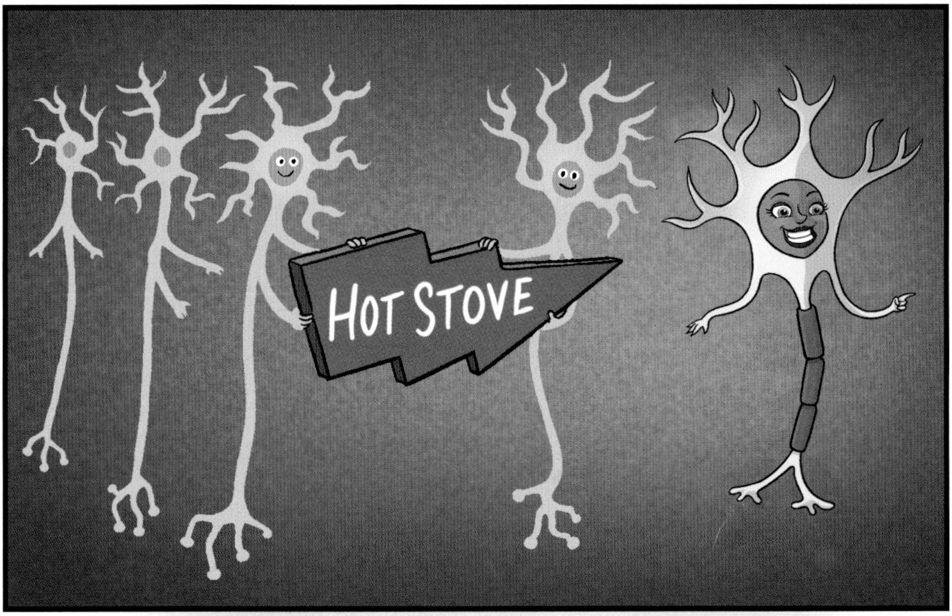
HOT STOVE

Messages carry information about touch, vision, hearing, taste, and smell.

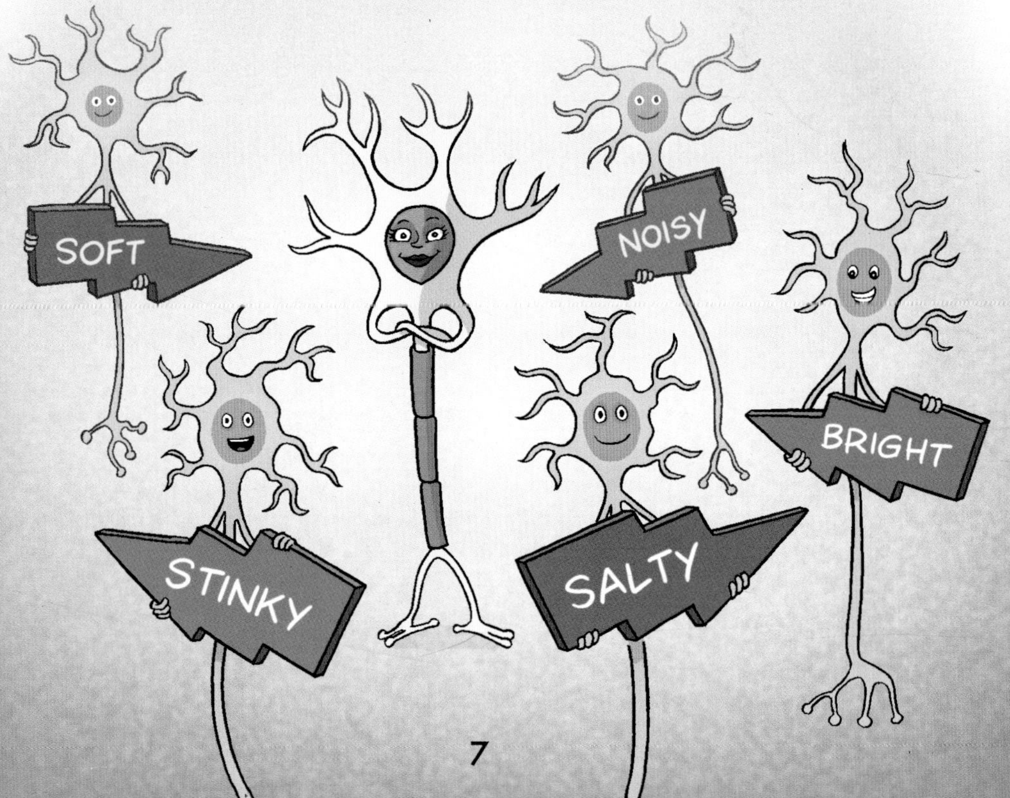
SOFT
NOISY
BRIGHT
STINKY
SALTY

Messages enter a neuron through dendrites.

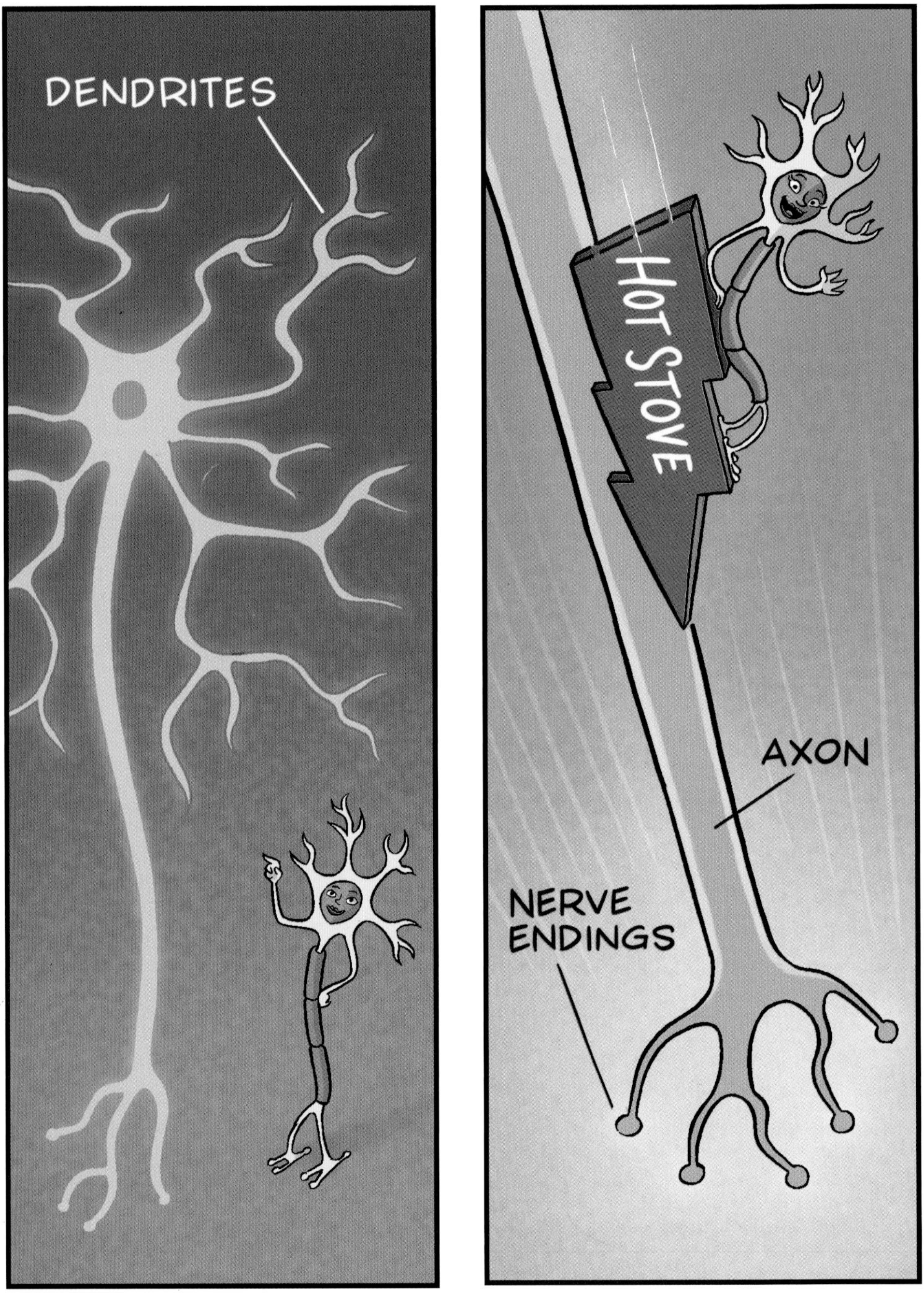
DENDRITES
HOT STOVE
AXON
NERVE ENDINGS

The axon sends the messages to the nerve endings.

To reach the next neuron, messages cross a synapse.

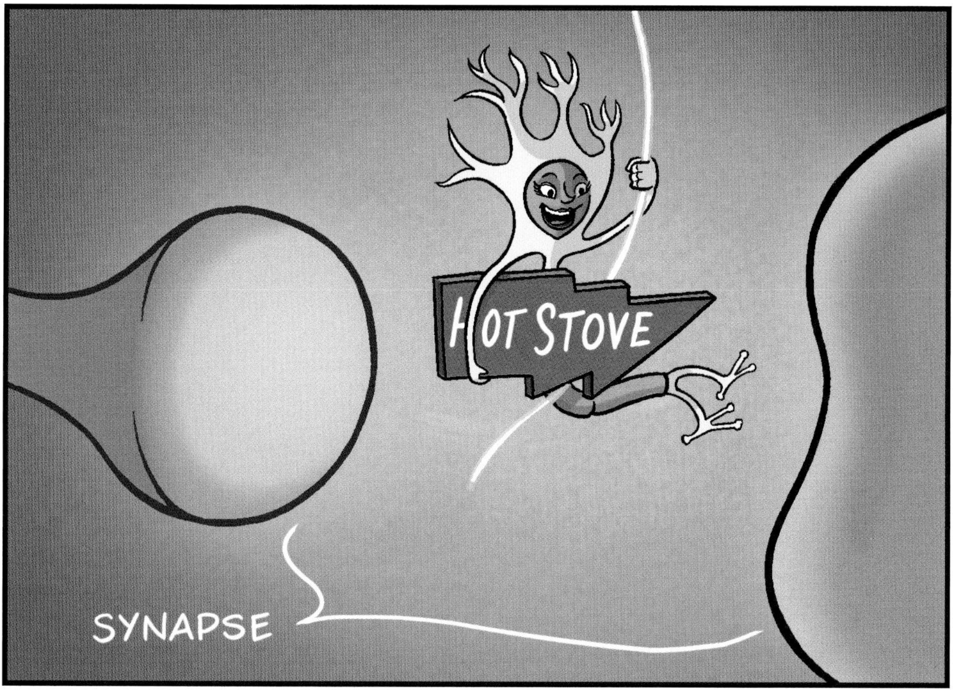
HOT STOVE
SYNAPSE

Chemicals carry messages over this gap.

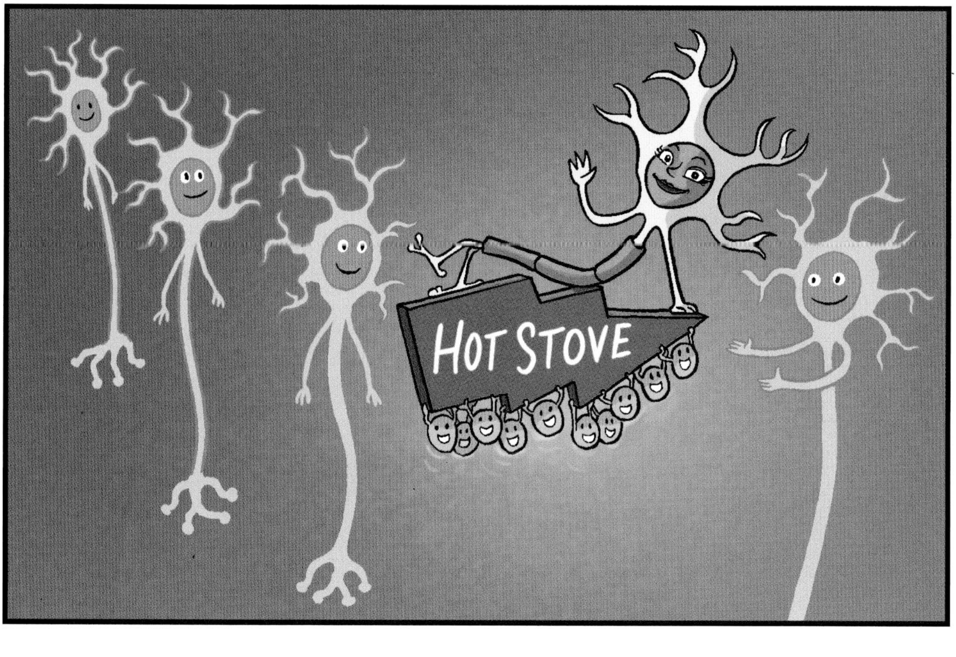
HOT STOVE

Neurons pass messages until they reach the spinal cord.

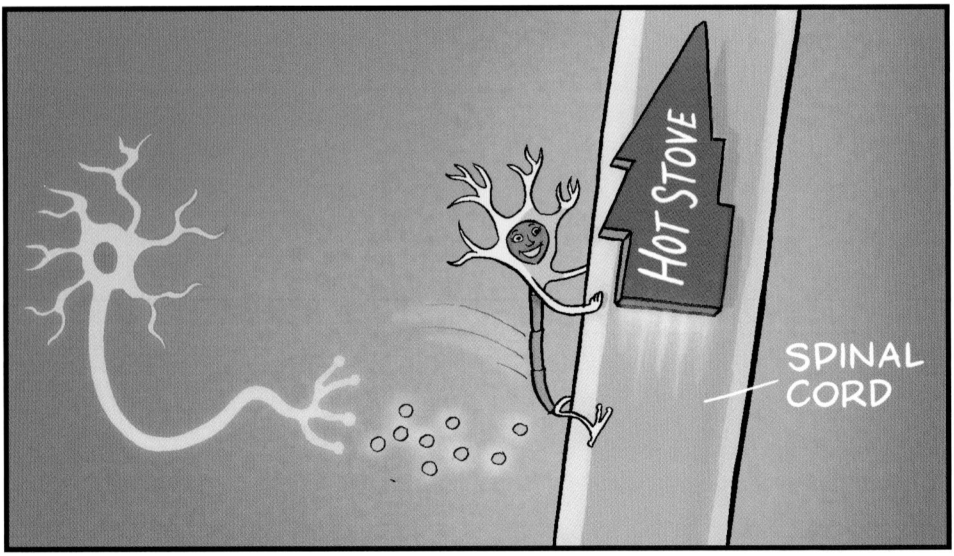
HOT STOVE
SPINAL CORD

This long rope of nerves runs up your back.

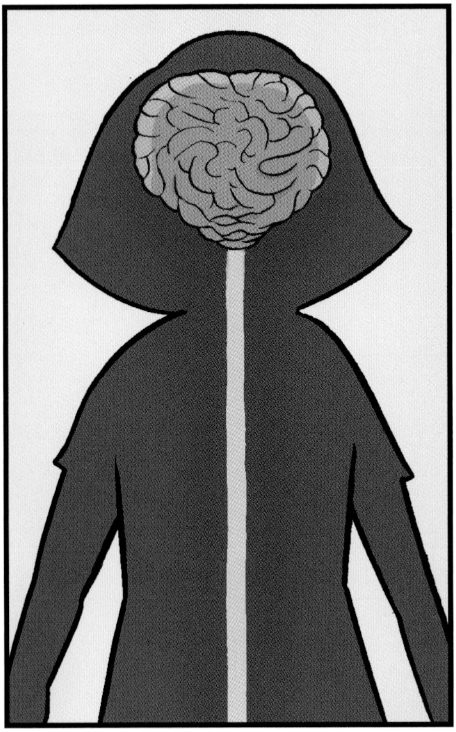

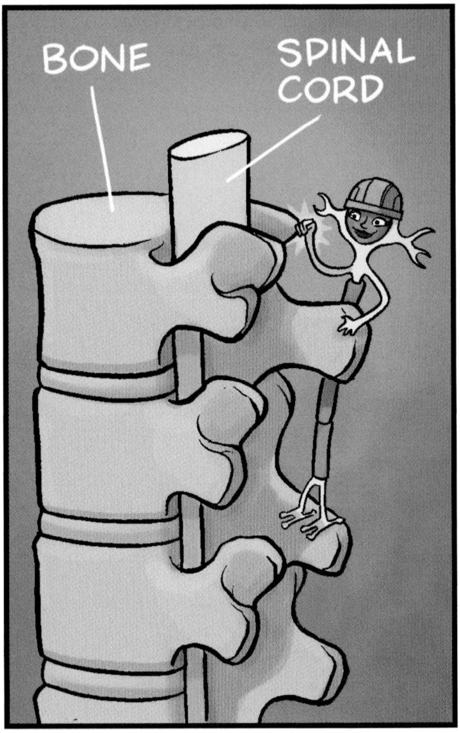
BONE
SPINAL CORD

Bones protect the spinal cord.

The spinal cord carries messages to and from the brain.

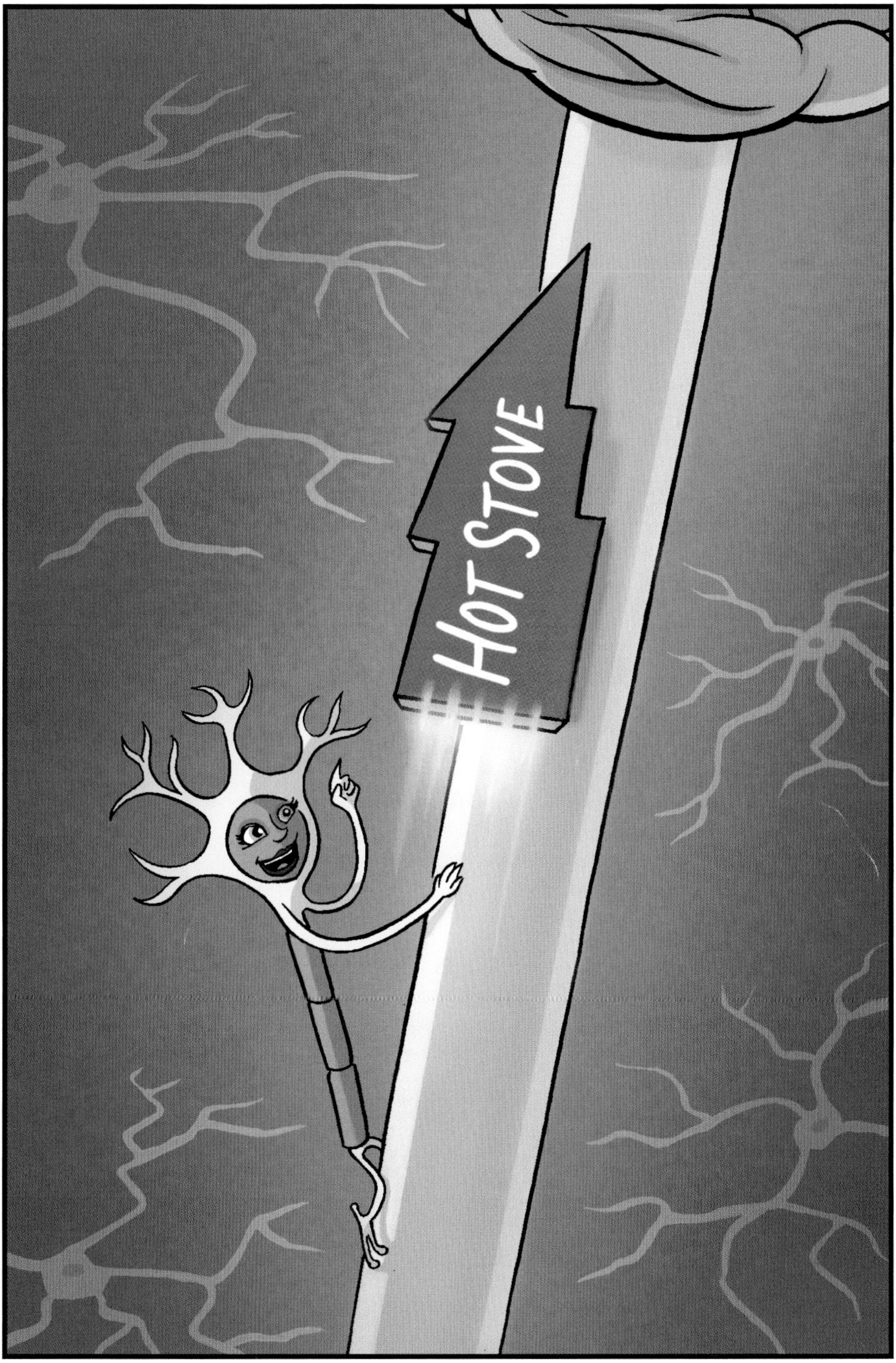
HOT STOVE

The Brain Is Boss

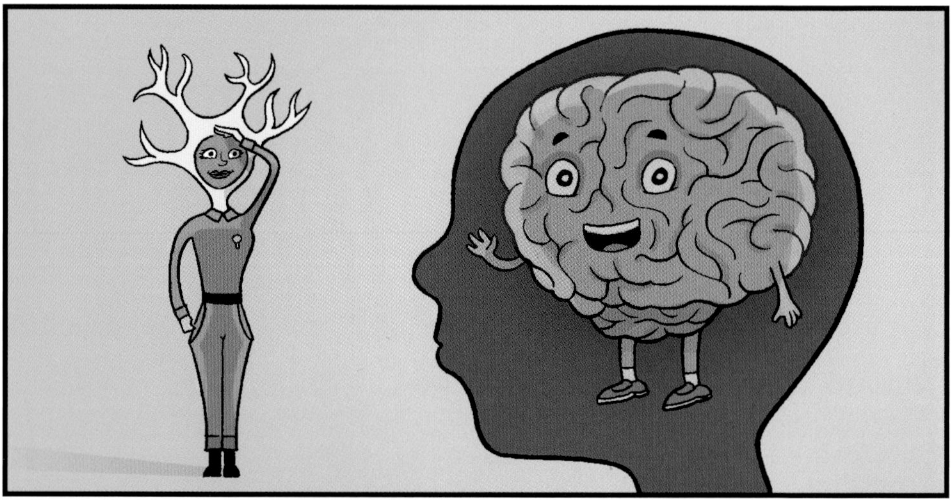

The brain is like a general. It is in charge of your body's nervous system.

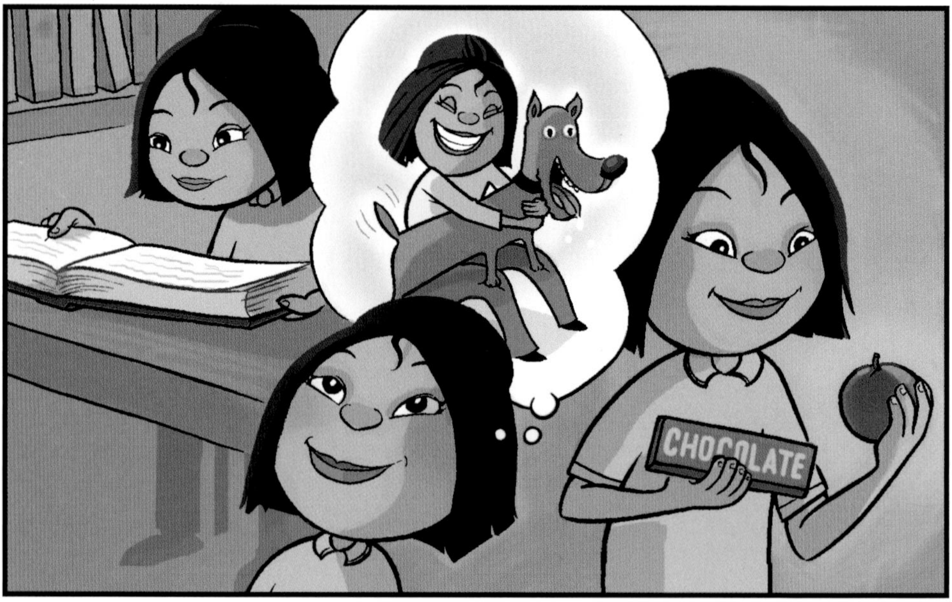

It helps you learn, store memories, and make decisions.

Ridges and grooves give the brain extra space for holding information.

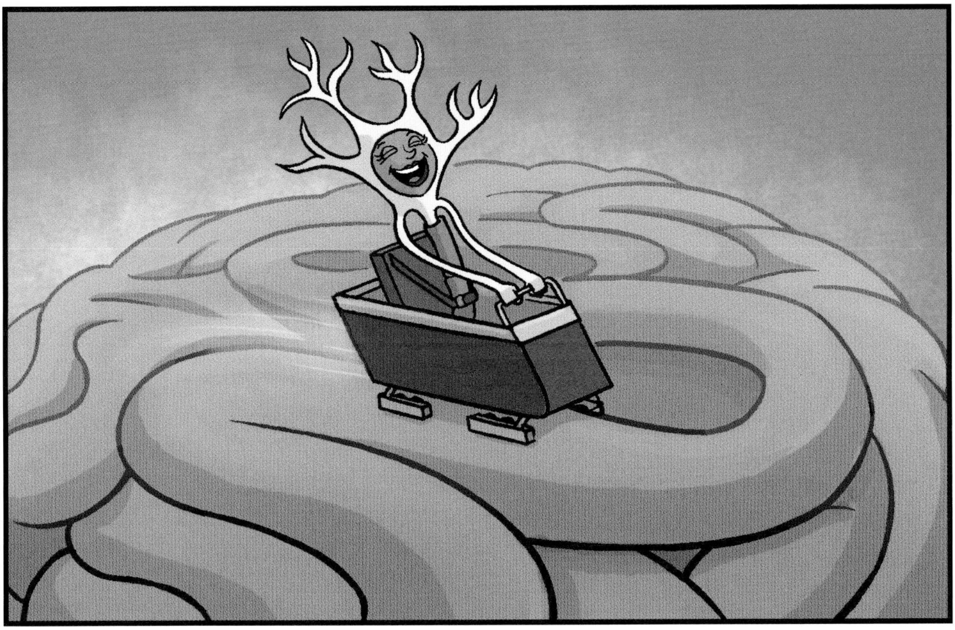

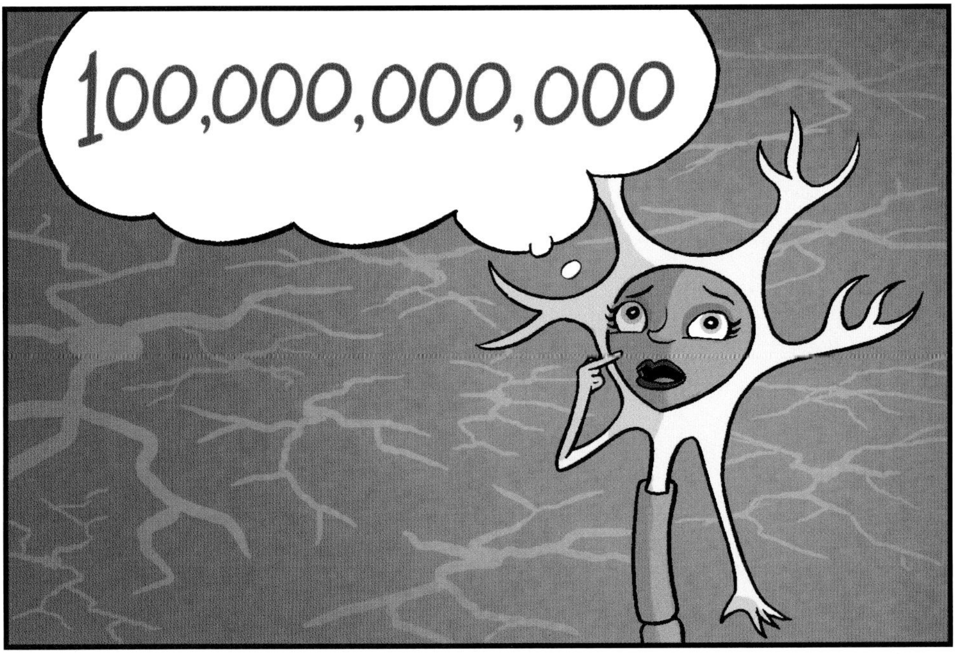
100,000,000,000

Packed inside the brain are more than 100 billion neurons.

The brain reviews all the messages it receives.

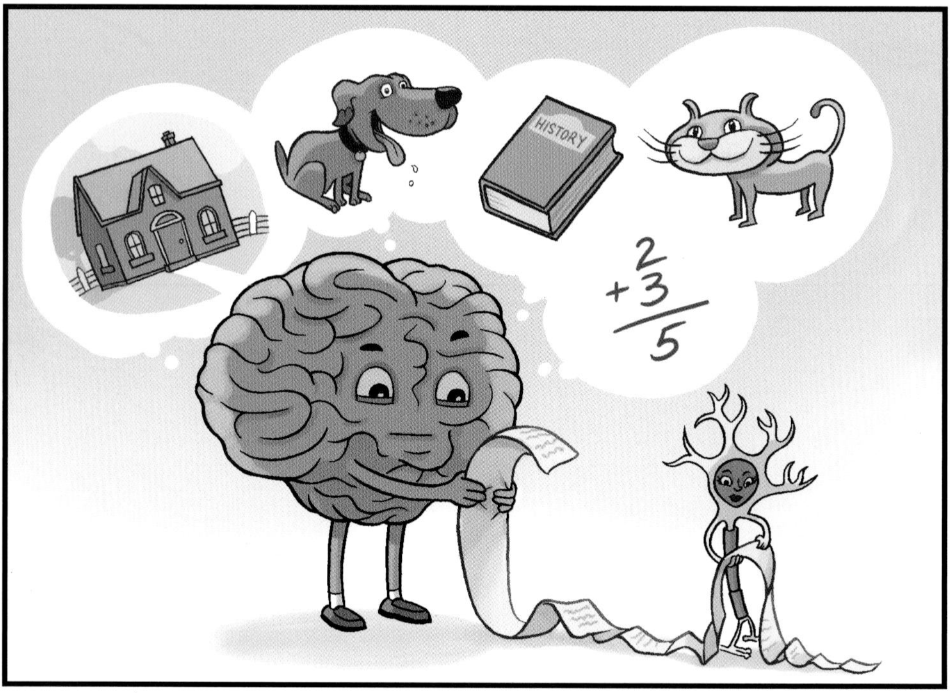
HISTORY
2
+3
5

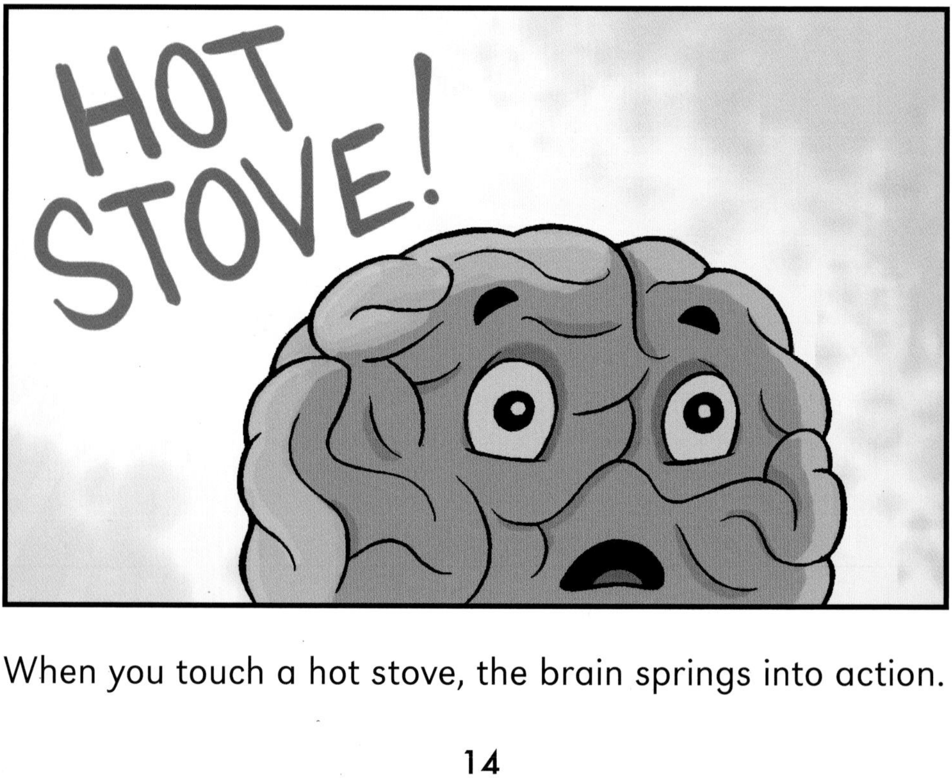
HOT STOVE!

When you touch a hot stove, the brain springs into action.

It sends a message to the neurons.

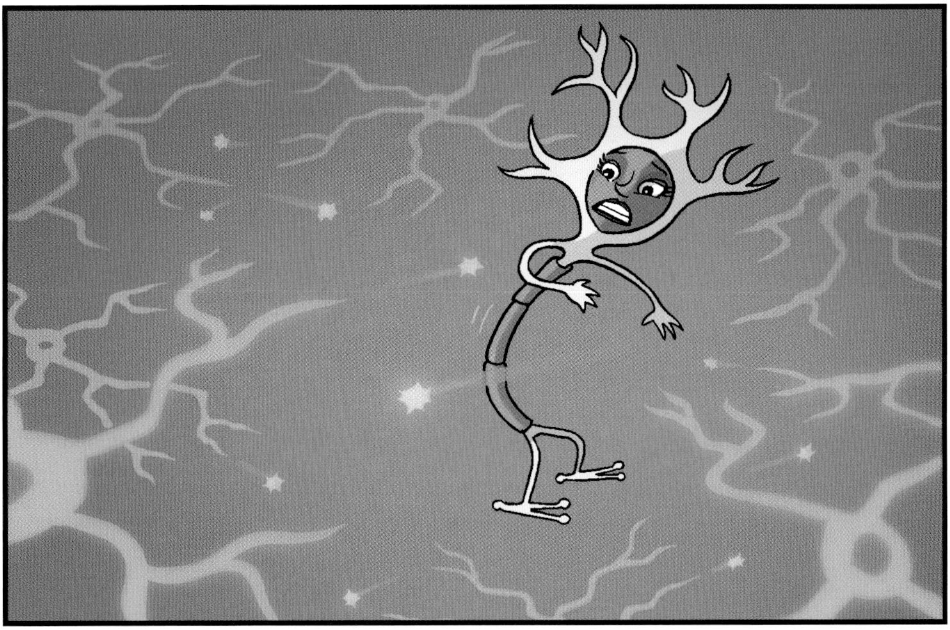

The message tells you to pull your hand away from the stove right away.

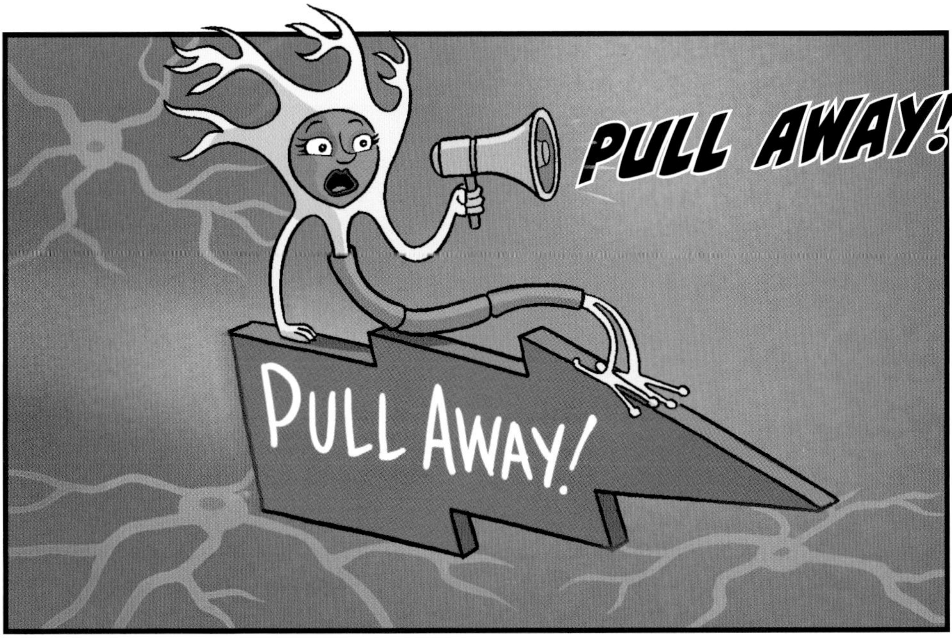
PULL AWAY!
PULL AWAY!

Spreading the Signal

The brain's message must now go to the right body part.

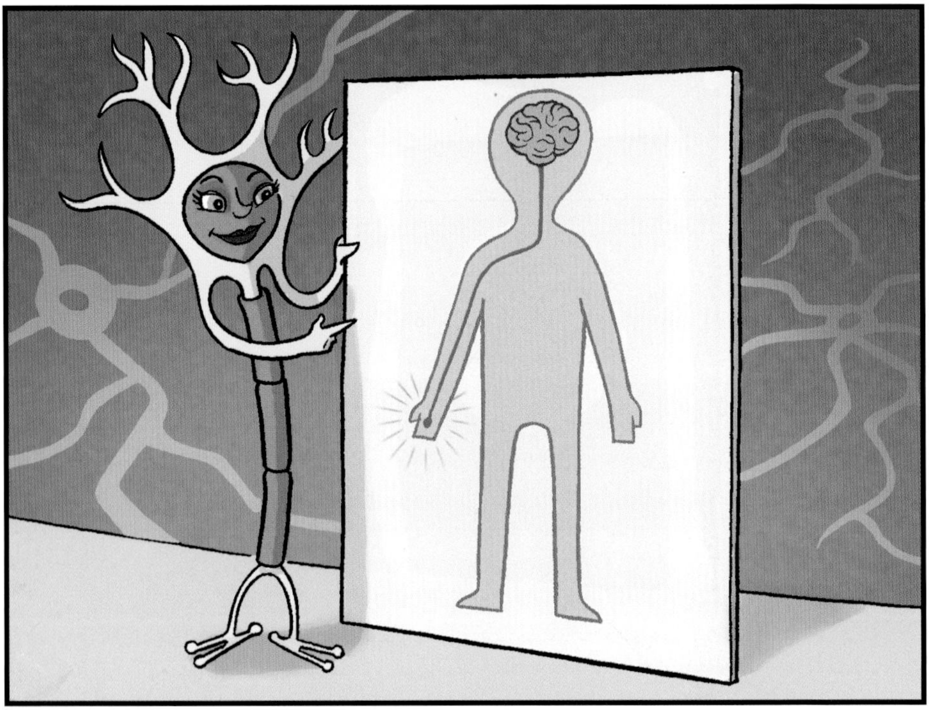

The message moves back down the spinal cord.

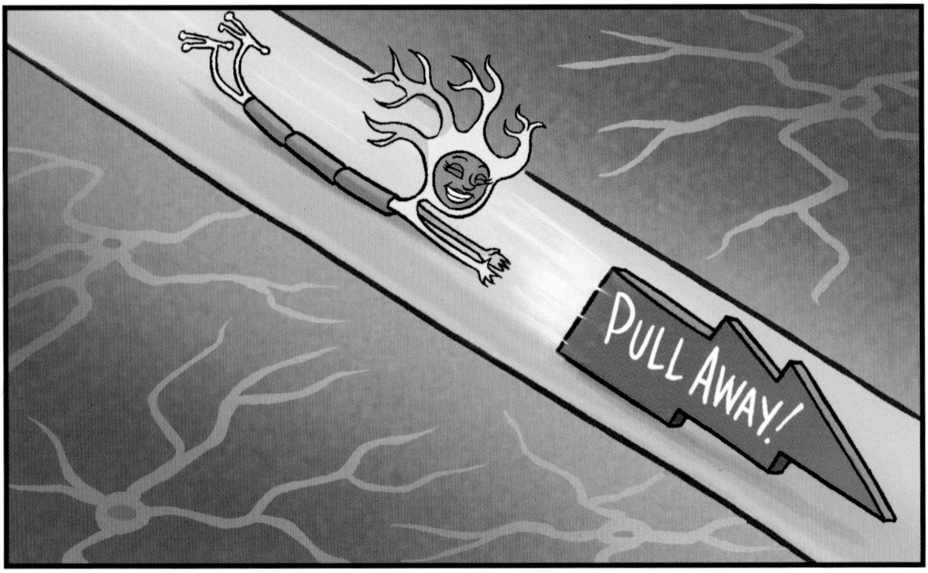
PULL AWAY!

Nerves link the spinal cord to every organ and muscle in the body.

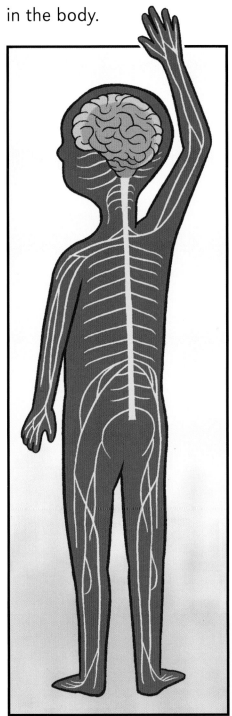

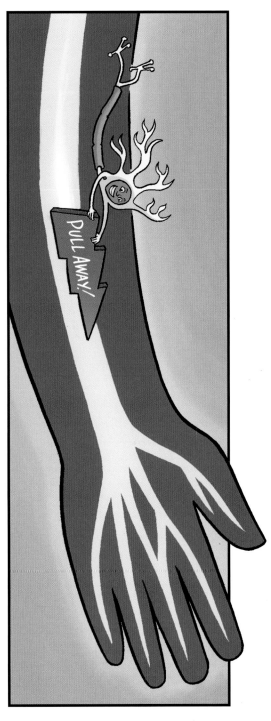

The message goes straight to where it's needed.

The brain's message reaches your hand.

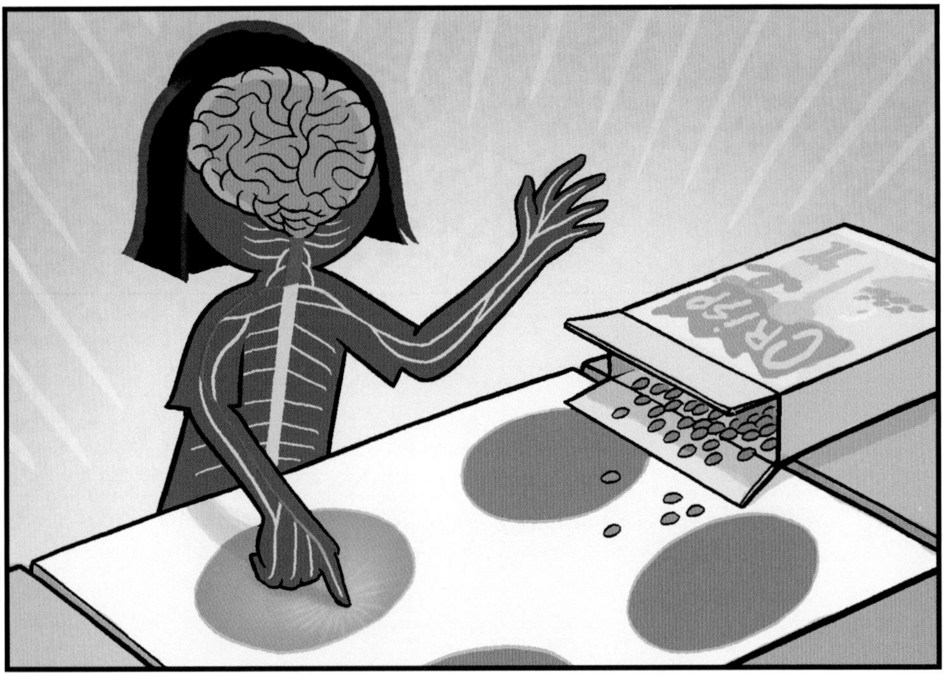

You pull it away from the stove.

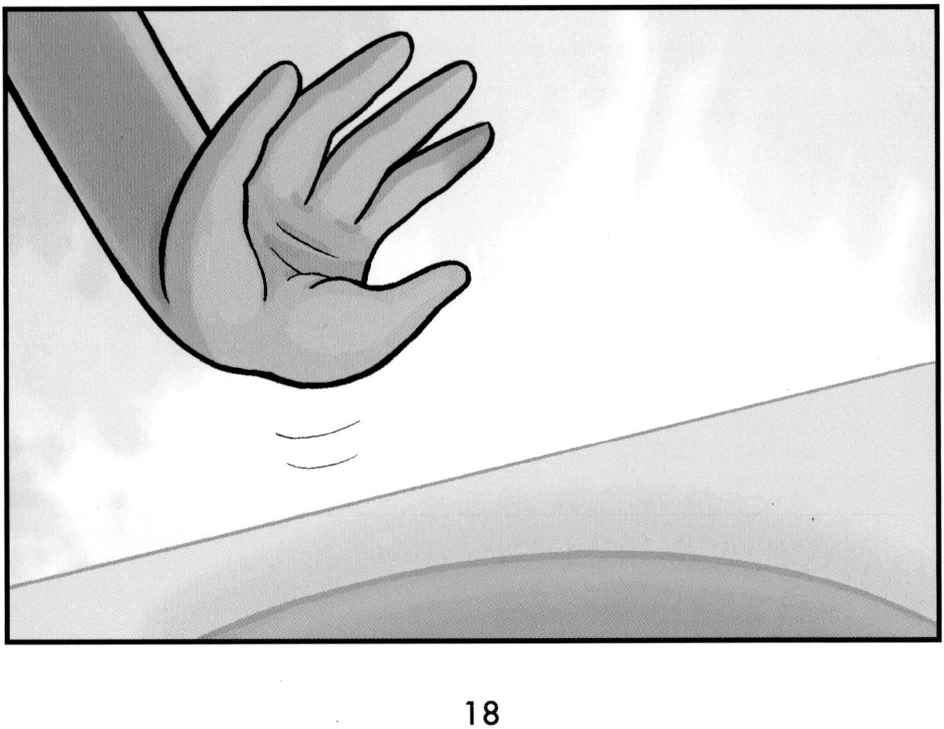

Of course, messages move much faster than you can read about them.

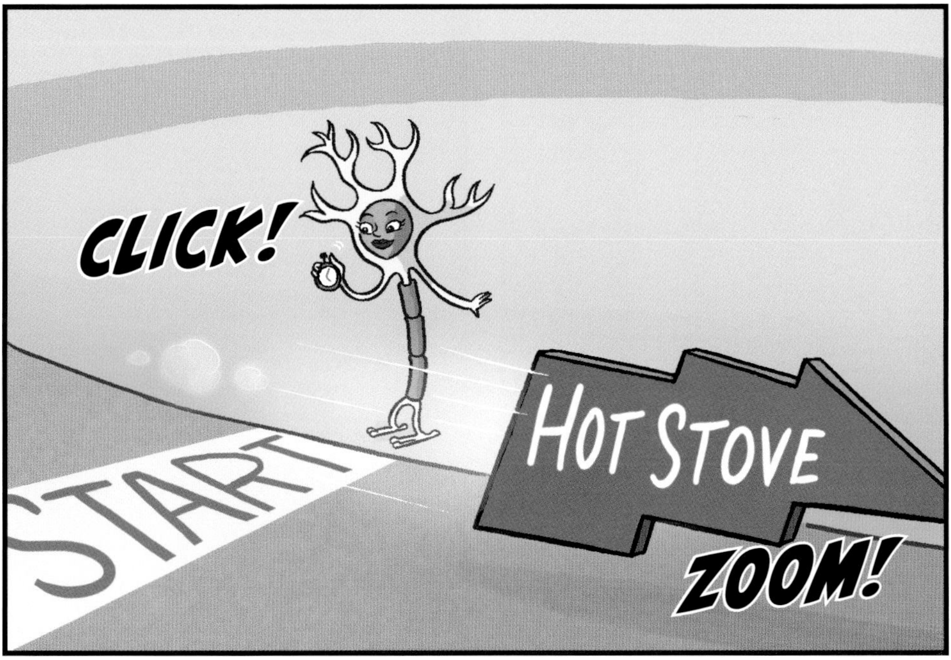
CLICK!
HOT STOVE
START
ZOOM!

They travel through your body in just a split second!

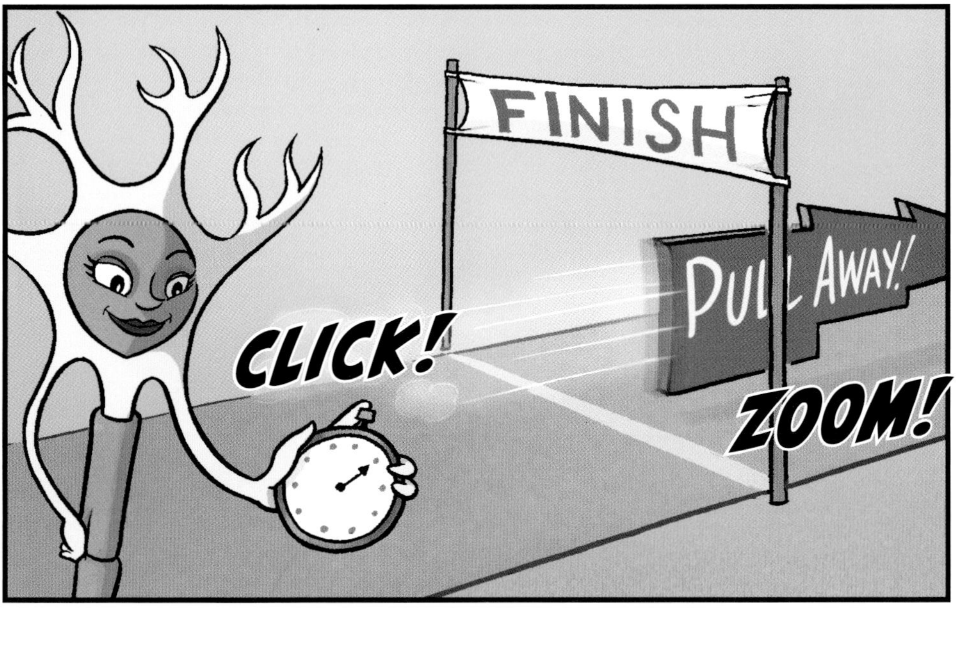
FINISH
CLICK!
PU L AWAY!
ZOOM!

The nervous system doesn't just control your muscles. It also keeps all of your body parts working.

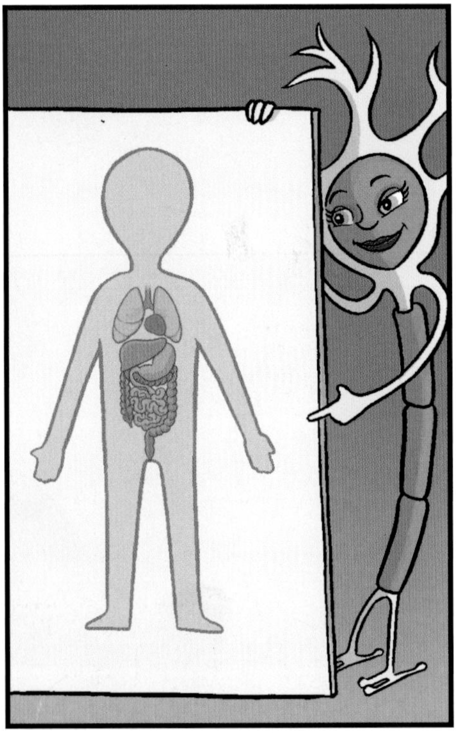

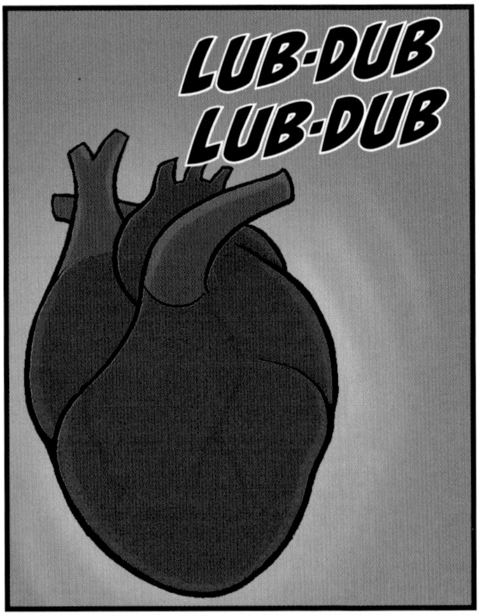
LUB-DUB
LUB-DUB

The nervous system tells your heart to beat.

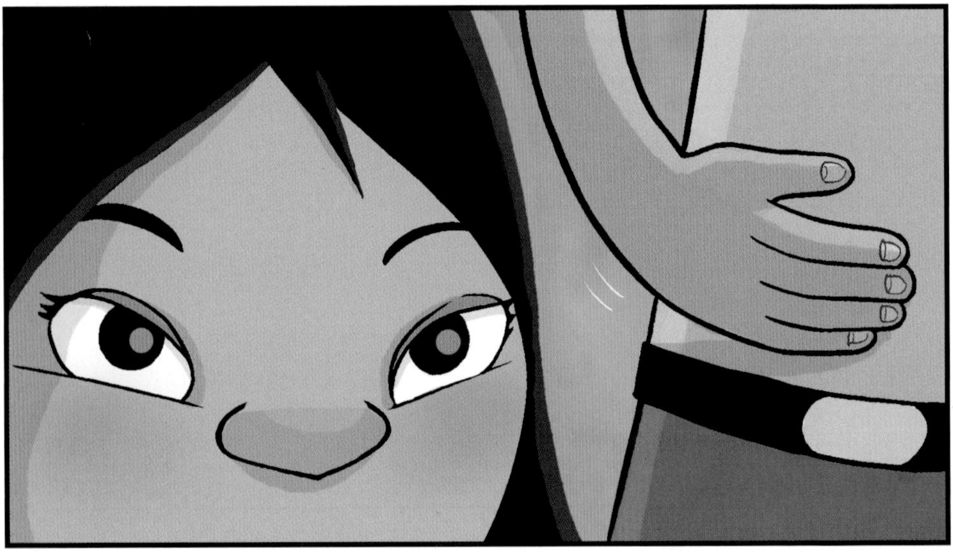

It tells your eyes to blink and your stomach to digest food.

The nervous system has many important jobs. Some keep you safe. Others help you have fun.

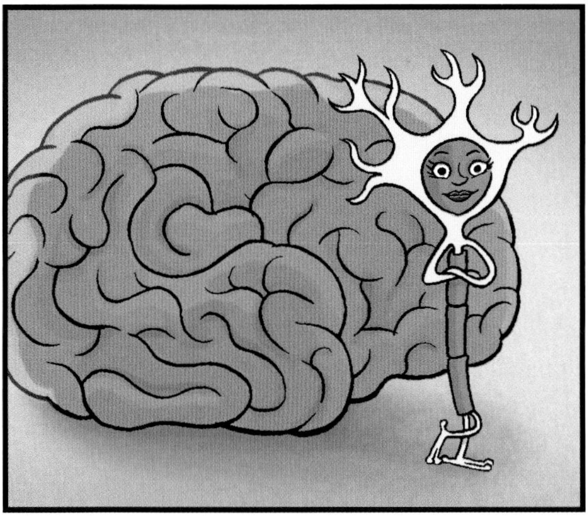

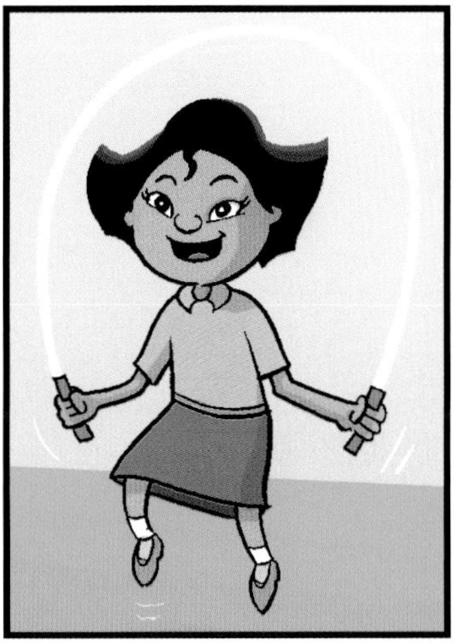

Why, your nervous system even helped you read this book!

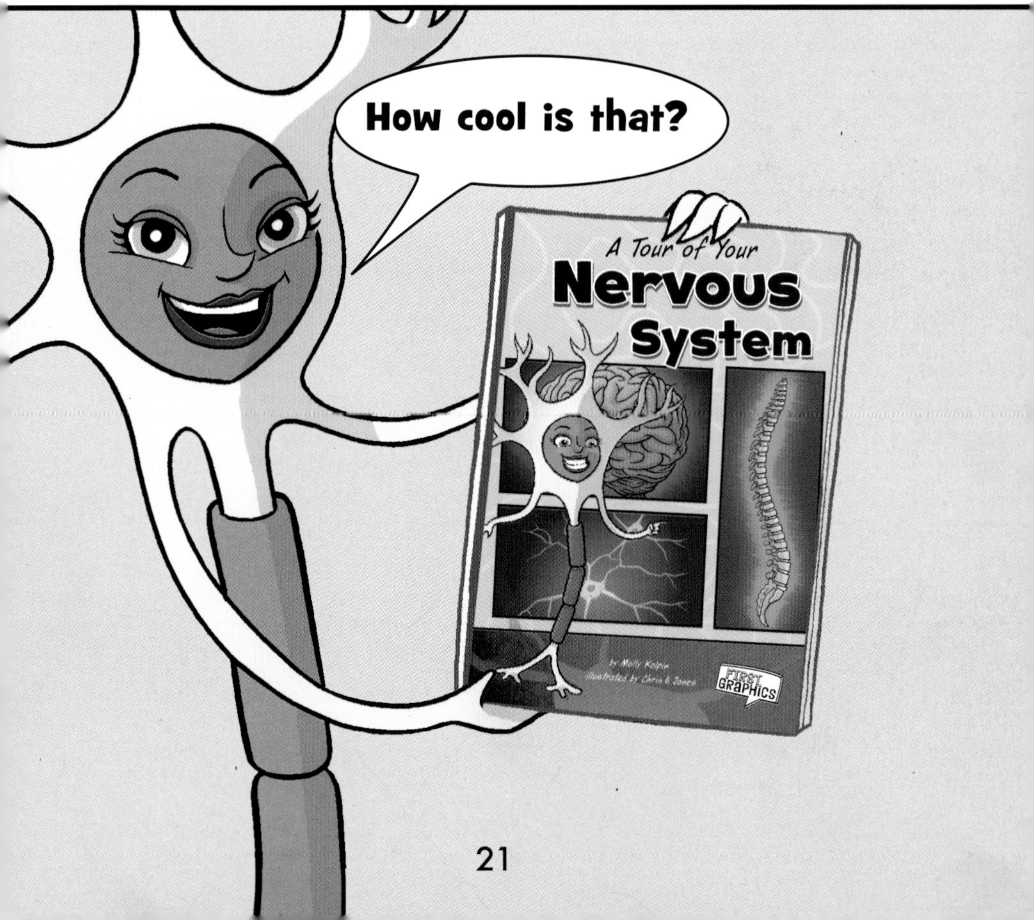
How cool is that?
A Tour of Your
Nervous System
FIRST GRAPHICS

Glossary

axon—arm of a nerve cell that sends out signals

cell—a basic part of an animal or plant that is so small you can't see it without a microscope

dendrite—arm of a nerve cell that receives signals

digest—to break down food so it can be used by the body

neuron—nerve cell

organ—a body part that does a certain job

spinal cord—a strip of tissue that connects to the brain and runs down along the back, inside the backbone; the spinal cord carries messages between the brain and nerves

synapse—the place where a message passes from one neuron to the next

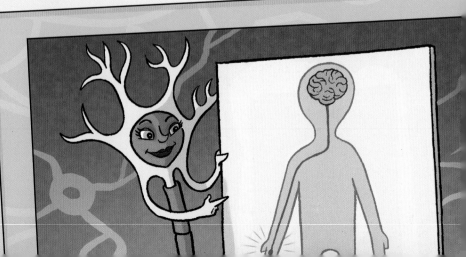

Read More

Burstein, John. *The Astounding Nervous System: How Does My Brain Work?* Slim Goodbody's Body Buddies. New York: Crabtree Pub., 2009.

Niver, Heather Moore. *The Nervous System.* The Human Body. New York: Gareth Stevens Pub., 2012.

Riley, Joelle. *Your Nervous System.* How Does Your Body Work? Minneapolis: Lerner Publications Co., 2013.

Internet Sites

FactHound offers a safe, fun way to find Internet sites related to this book. All of the sites on FactHound have been researched by our staff.

Here's all you do:

Visit *www.facthound.com*

Type in this code: 9781429687393

Check out projects, games and lots more at
www.capstonekids.com

Index

Titles in this set:

A Tour of Your
Circulatory System

A Tour of Your
Digestive System

A Tour of Your
Muscular and
Skeletal Systems

A Tour of Your
Nervous System

A Tour of Your
Respiratory System